# Picture Patterns
## Two Pictures

Name

Date

W9-CED-184

**To parents**
Guide your child to write his or her name and date in the box above.
Do the exercise along with your child if he or she has difficulty.

■ Write a check mark (✓) above the picture that comes next in the pattern.

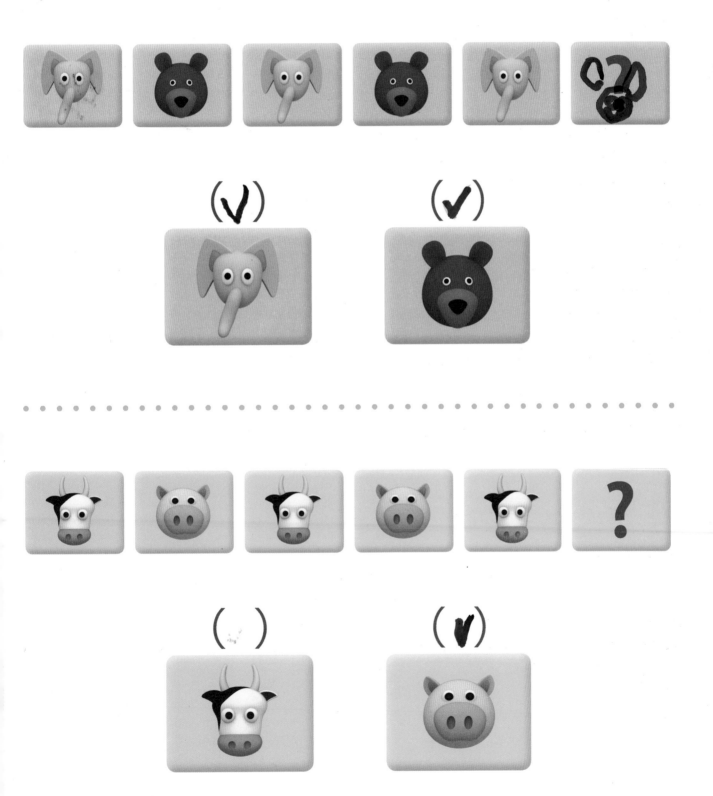

■ Write a check mark (✓) above the picture that comes next in the pattern.

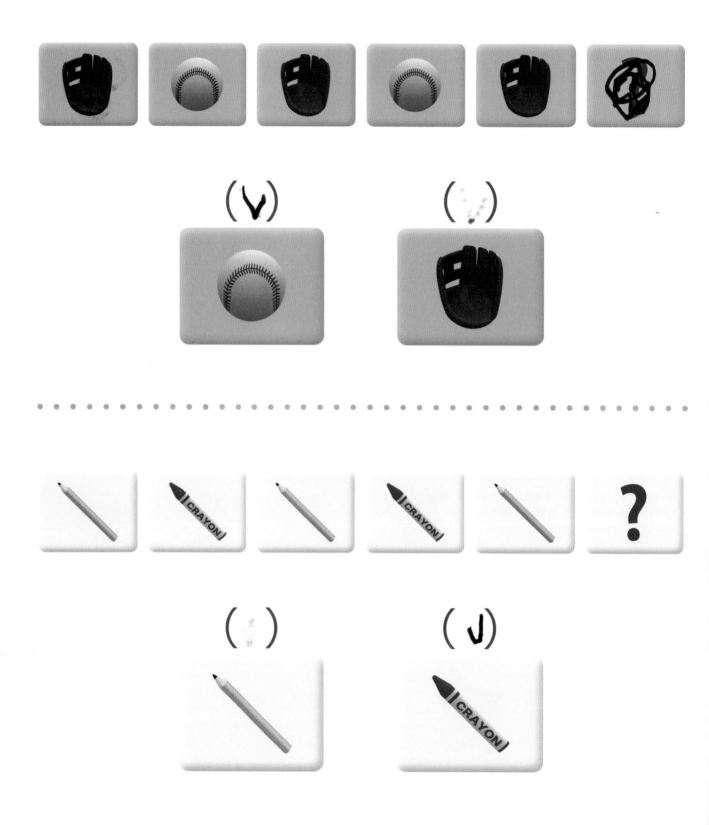

# Picture Patterns
## Two Pictures

**To parents**
The patterns are now arranged vertically. Guide your child to start with the top picture.

■ Write a check mark (✓) above the picture that comes next in the pattern.

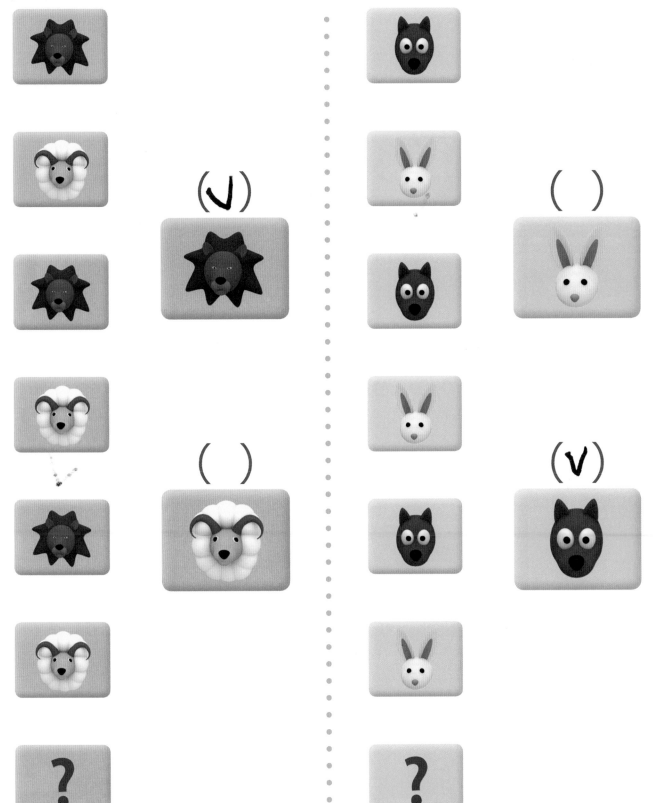

3

■ Write a check mark (✓) above the picture that comes next in the pattern.

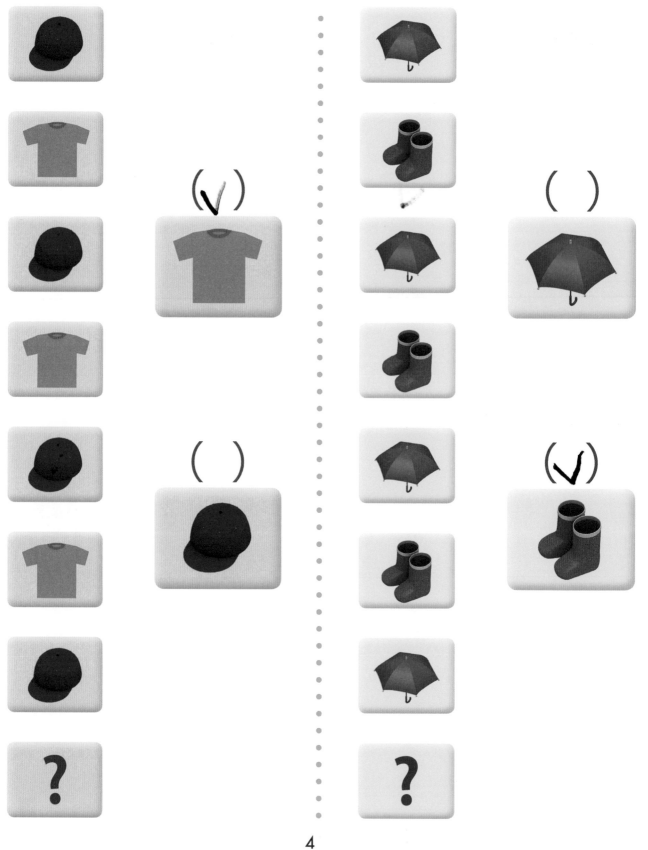

4

# Picture Patterns
## Three Pictures

Name

Date

**To parents**
Encourage your child to differentiate between the pictures.

■ Write a check mark (✓) above the picture that comes next in the pattern.

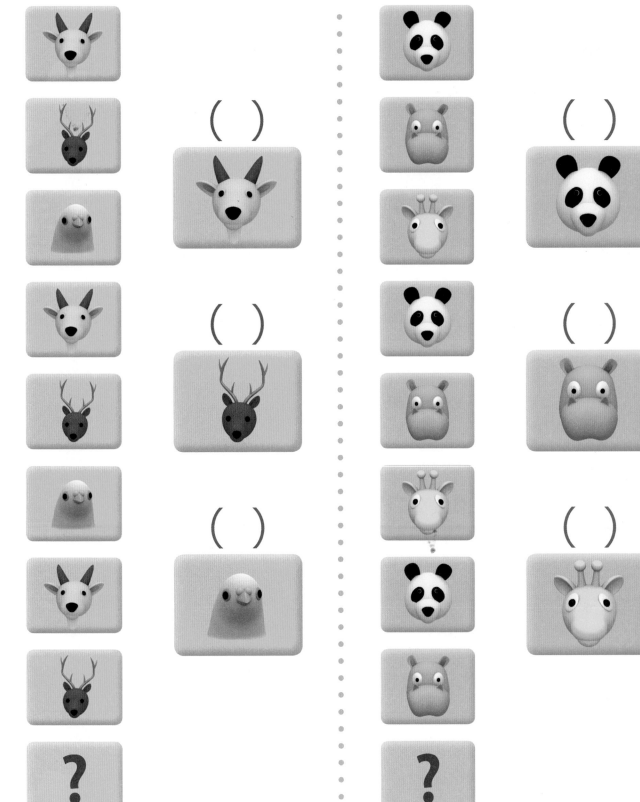

■ Write a check mark (✓) above the picture that comes next in the pattern.

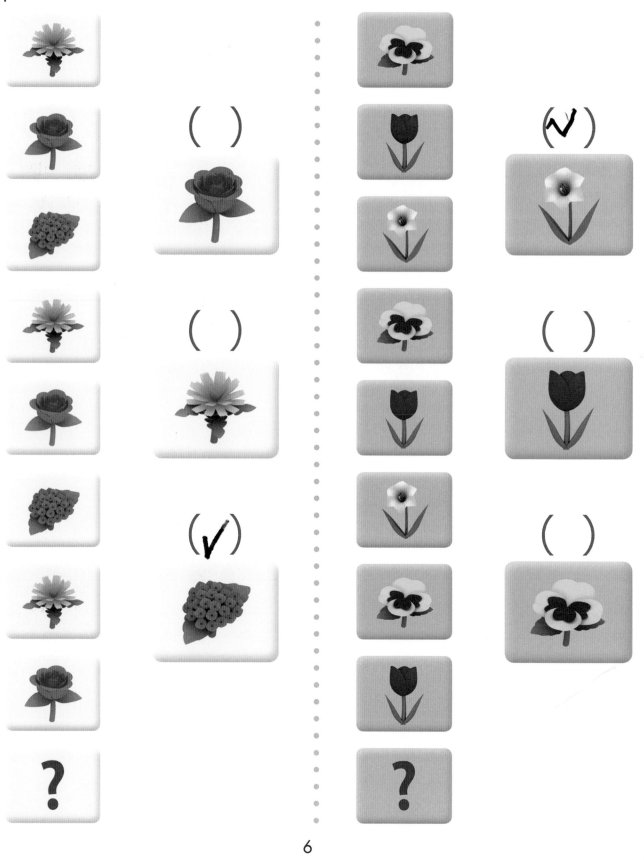

6

# Picture Patterns
Three Pictures

Name

Date

**To parents**
If your child has difficulty, encourage him or her to say the sequence of pictures out loud.

■ Write a check mark (✓) above the picture that comes next in the pattern.

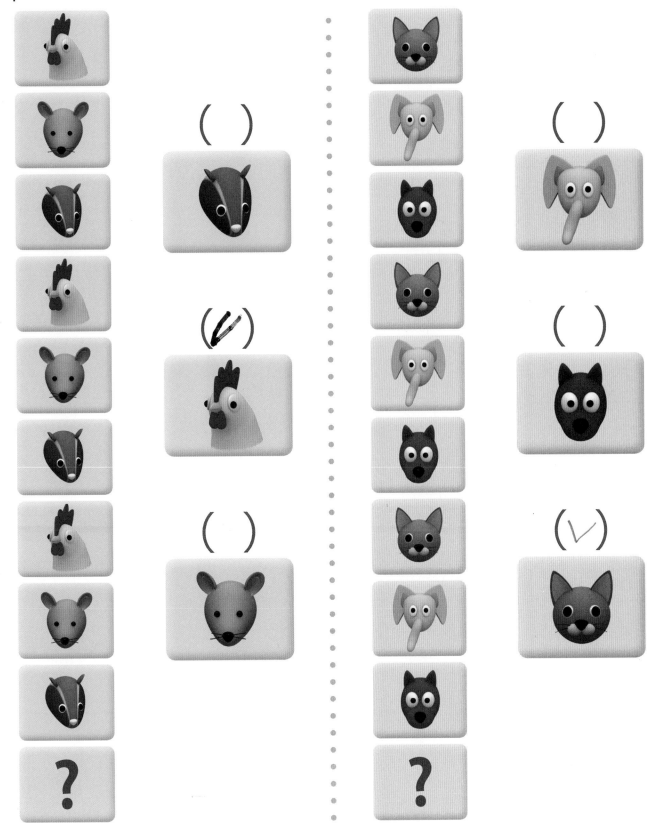

■ Write a check mark (✓) above the picture that comes next in the pattern.

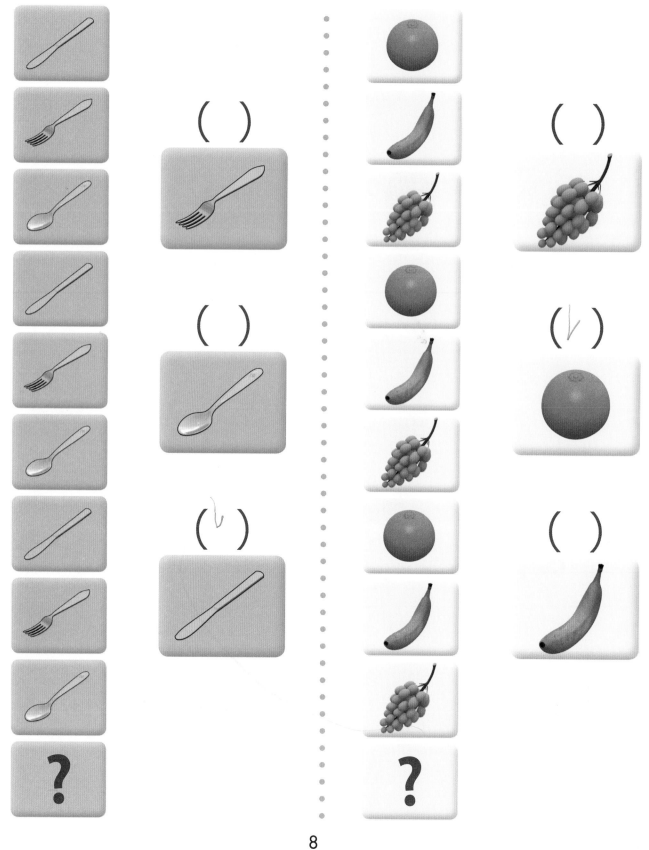

# Picture Patterns
## Two Shapes

Name

Date

**To parents**
The patterns are now made up of geometric shapes. Encourage
your child to differentiate between the shapes.

■ Write a check mark (✓) above the picture that comes next in the
pattern.

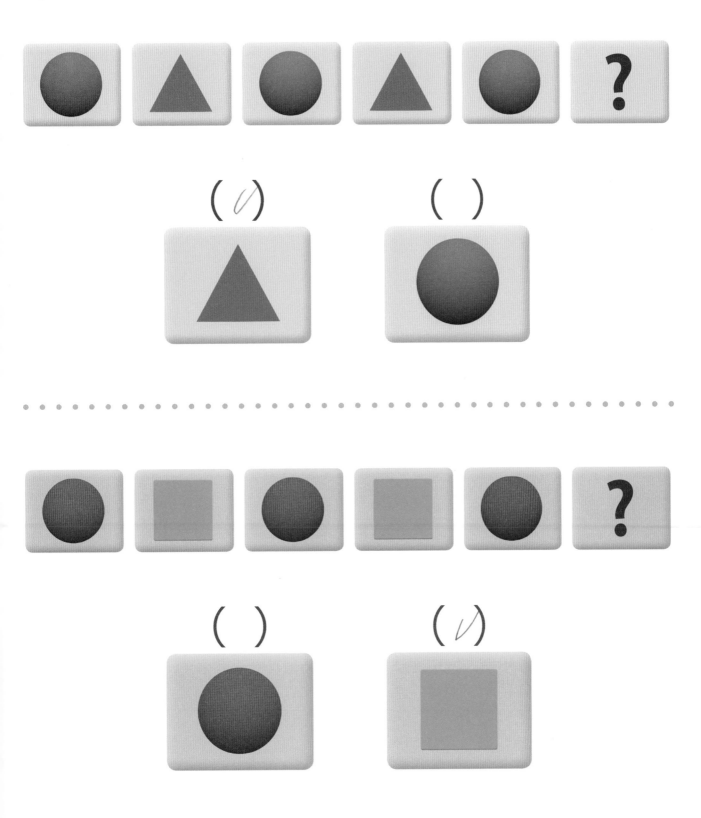

■ Write a check mark (✓) above the picture that comes next in the pattern.

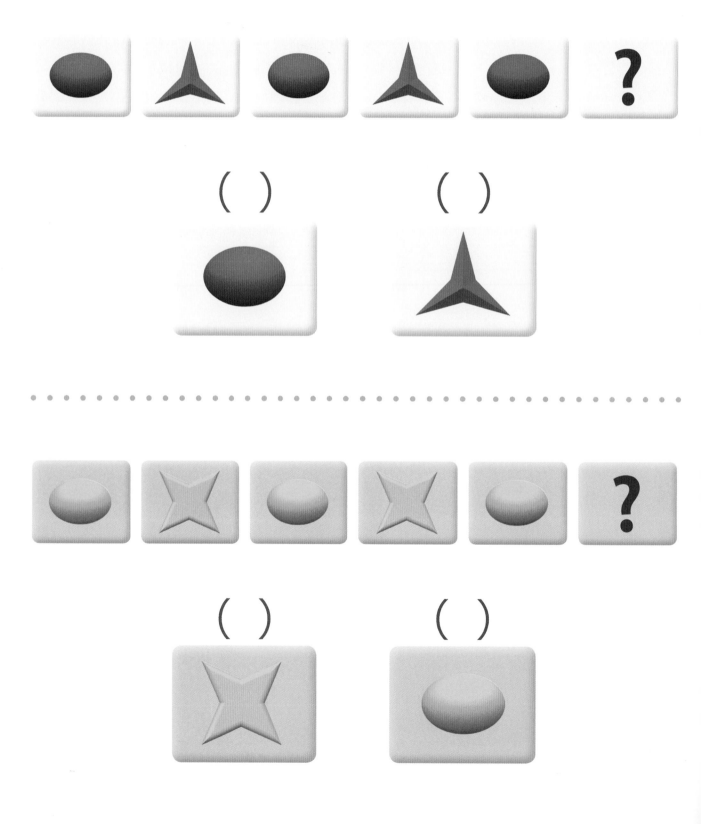

# Picture Patterns
## Two Shapes

Name

Date

**To parents**
If your child has difficulty, ask him or her to describe the two different shapes in the sequence.

■ Write a check mark (✓) above the picture that comes next in the pattern.

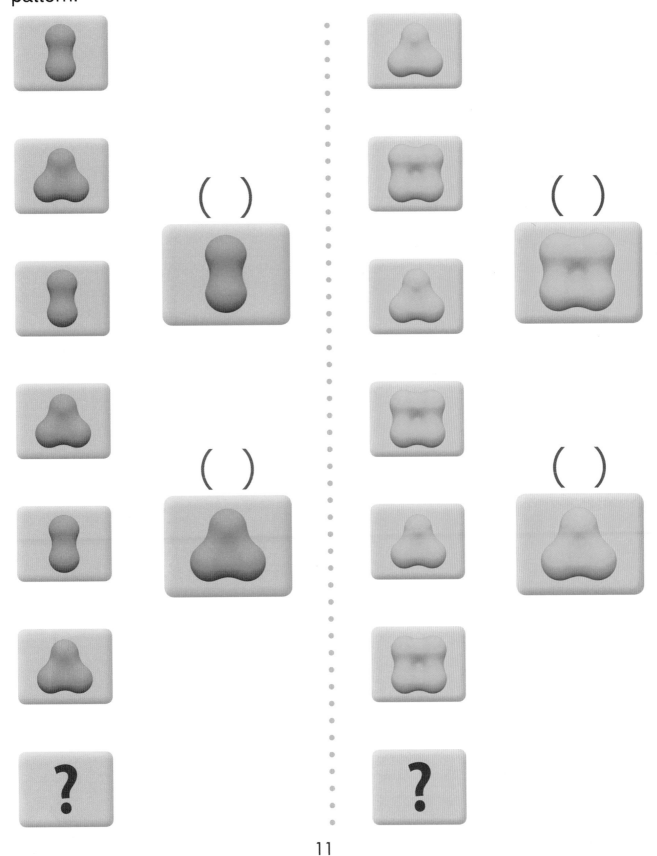

■ Write a check mark (✓) above the picture that comes next in the pattern.

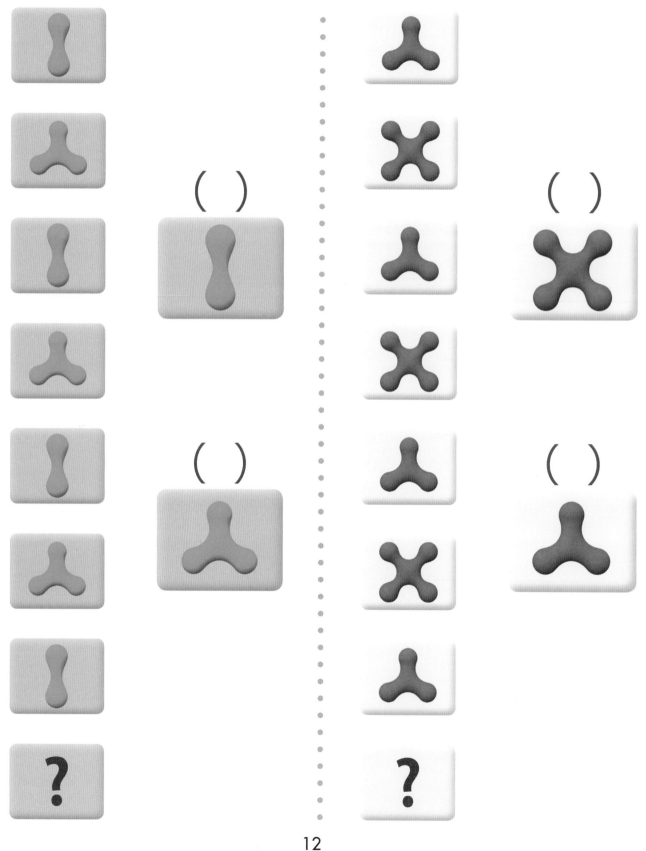

12

# Picture Patterns
## Three Shapes

Name

Date

**To parents**
The patterns are now made up of three shapes. Encourage
your child to differentiate between the shapes.

■ Write a check mark (✓) above the picture that comes next in the
pattern.

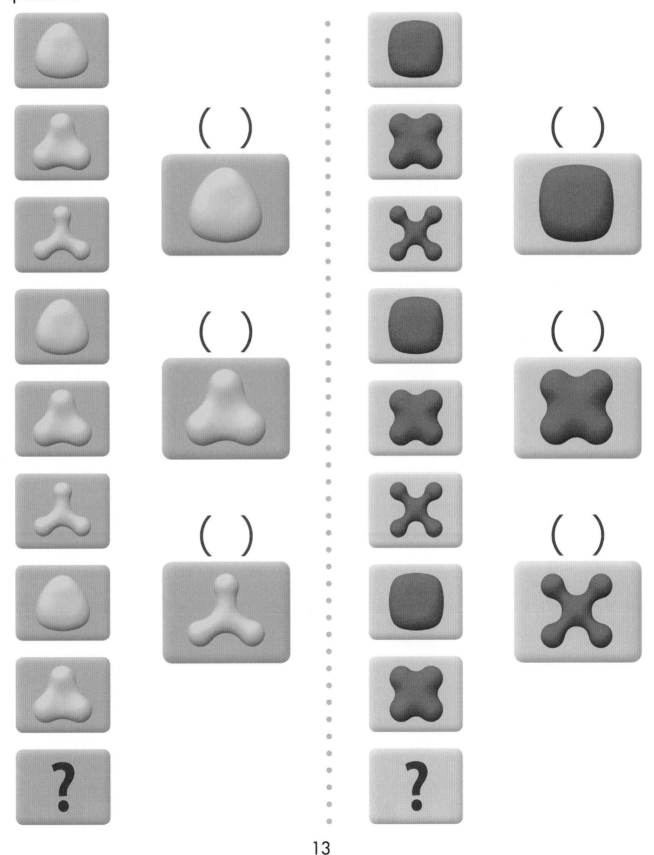

13

■ Write a check mark (✓) above the picture that comes next in the pattern.

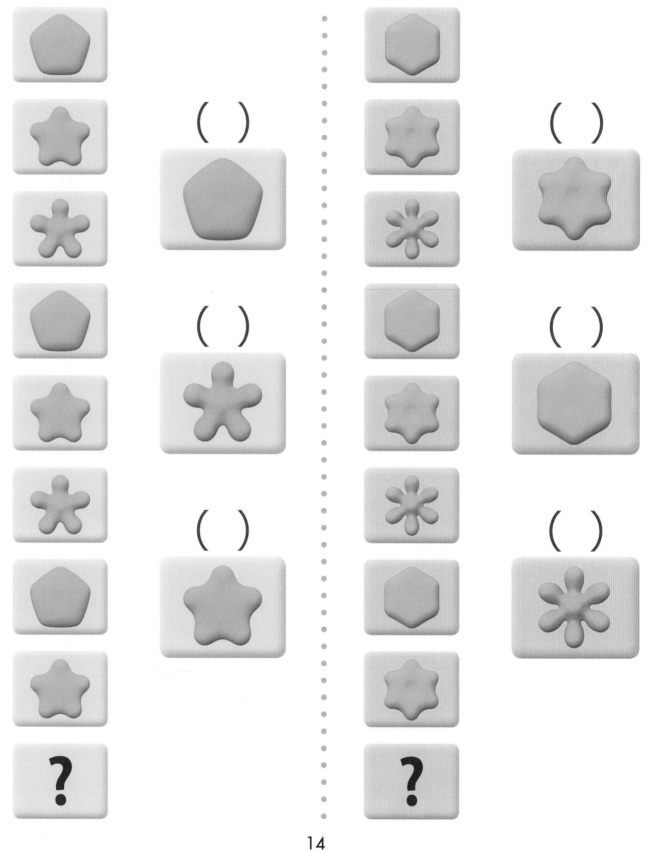

14

# Picture Patterns

Three Shapes

**To parents**
If your child has difficulty, encourage him or her to compare the center parts of the shapes.

■ Write a check mark (✓) above the picture that comes next in the pattern.

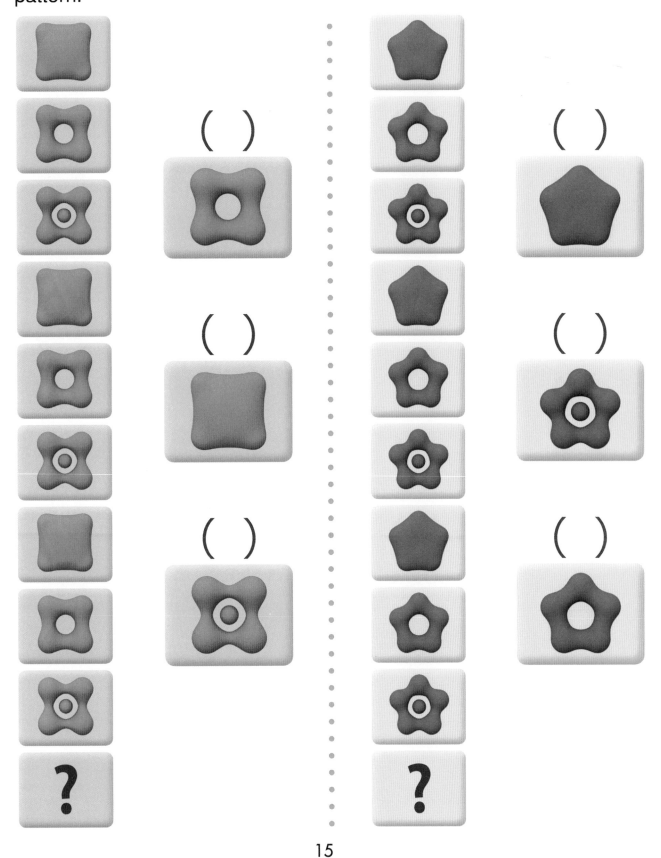

■ Write a check mark (✓) above the picture that comes next in the pattern.

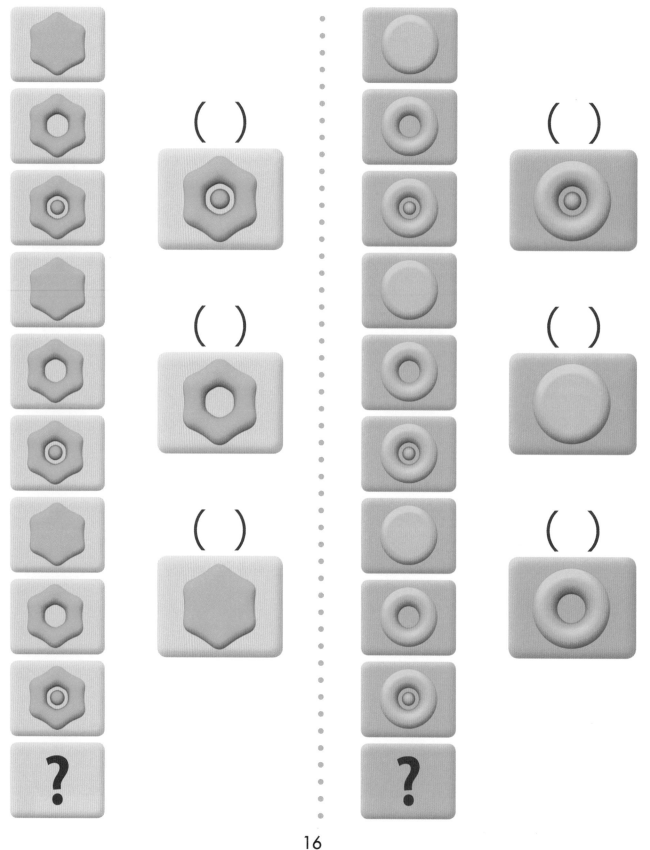

# Picture Patterns
## Three Pictures

Name

Date

**To parents**
The patterns are now more complicated. Encourage your child
to look carefully to find the end of each sequence.

■ Write a check mark (✓) above the picture that comes next in the
pattern.

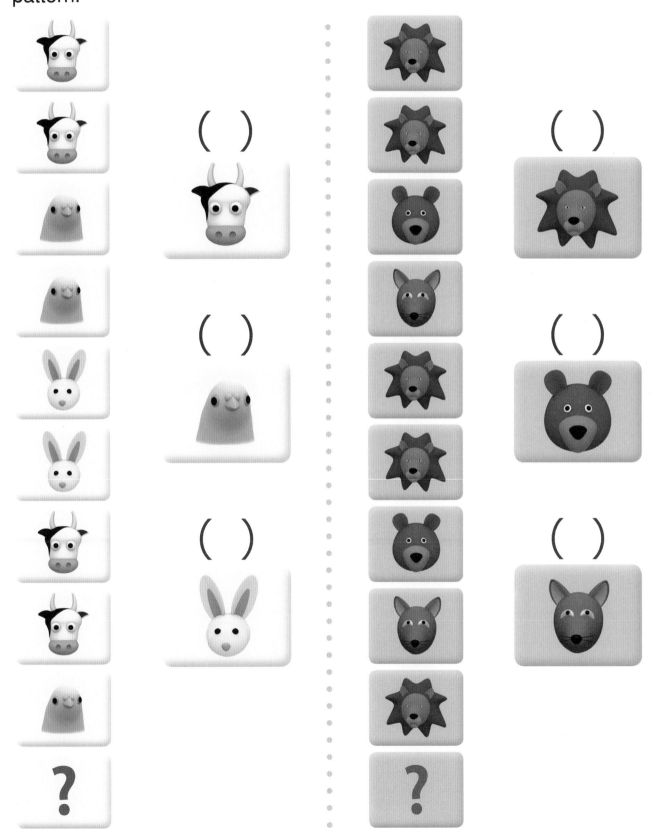

17

■ Write a check mark (✓) above the picture that comes next in the pattern.

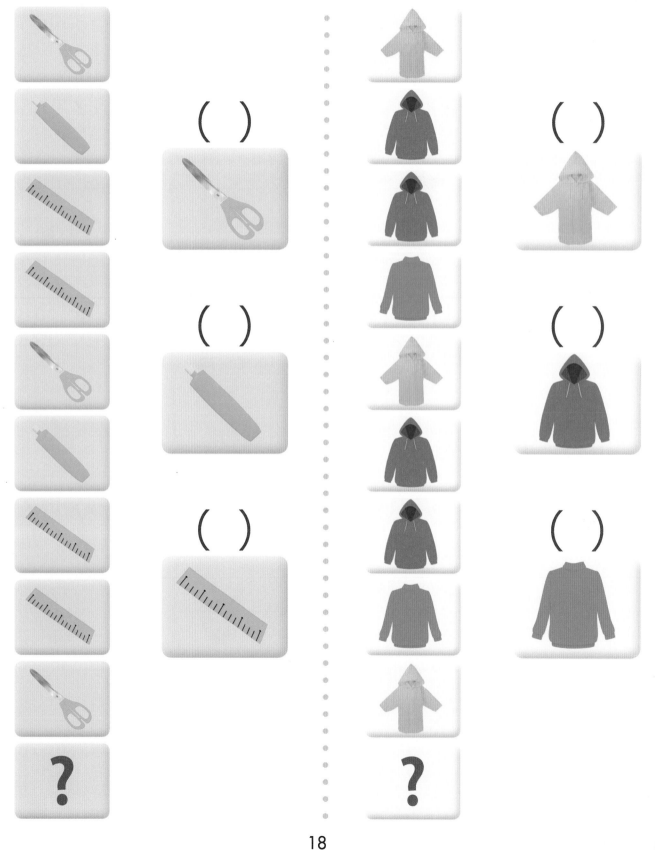

18

# Picture Patterns
Three Pictures

Name

Date

**To parents**
If your child has difficulty, encourage him or her to say the sequence of pictures out loud.

■ Write a check mark (✓) above the picture that comes next in the pattern.

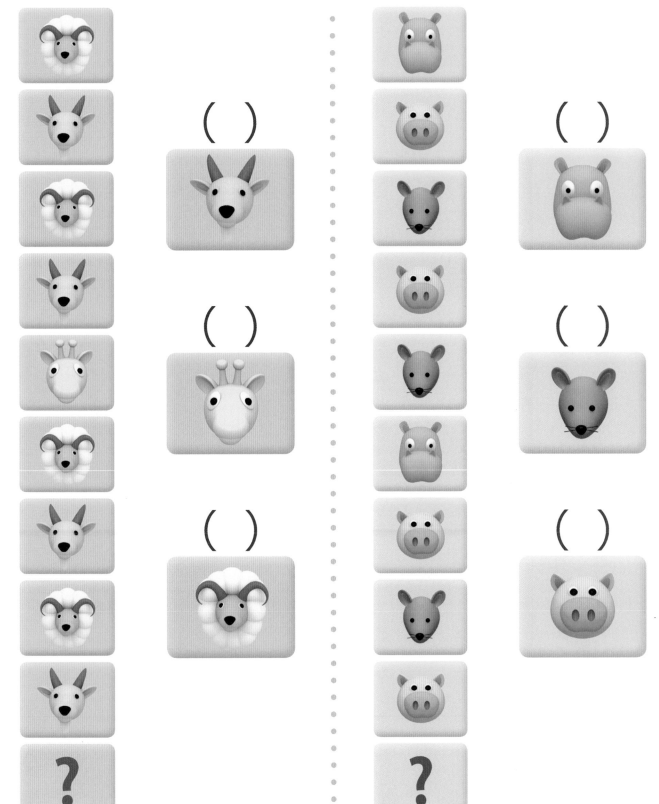

19

■ Write a check mark (✓) above the picture that comes next in the pattern.

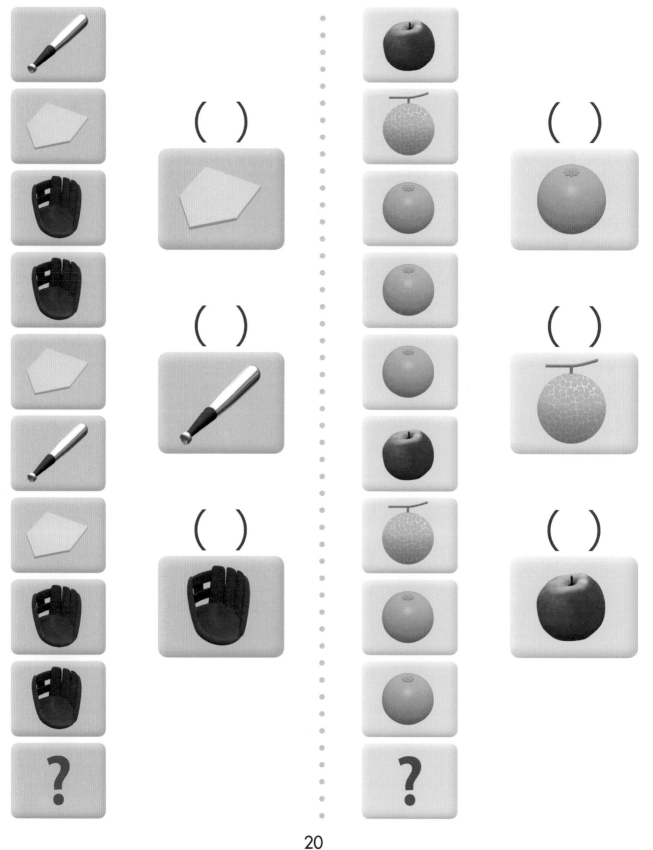

20

# Picture Patterns

## Three Shapes

Name

Date

**To parents**
The patterns are now made up of geometric shapes. Encourage
your child to differentiate between the shapes.

■ Write a check mark (✓) above the picture that comes next in the
pattern.

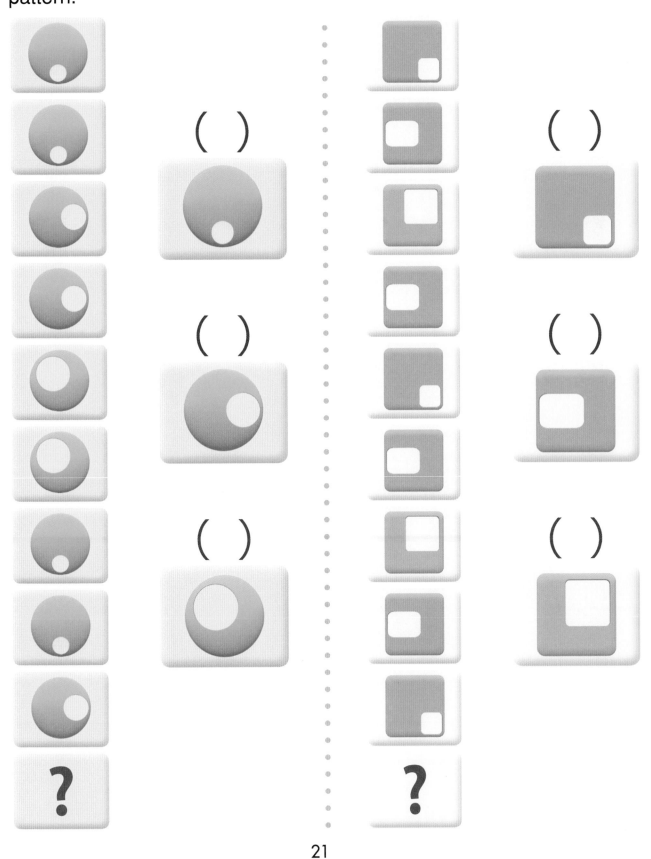

■ Write a check mark (✓) above the picture that comes next in the pattern.

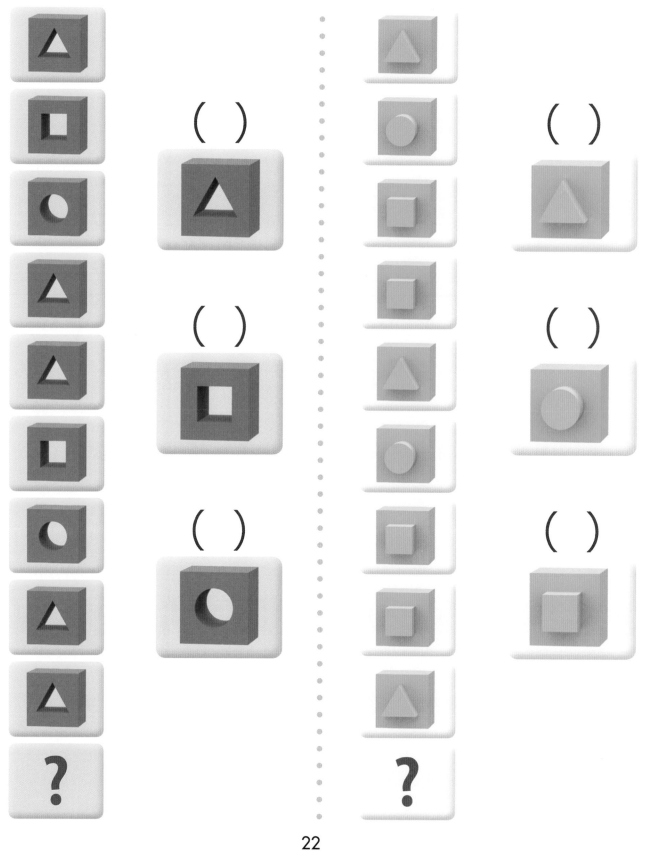

22

Name

Date

**To parents**
It is okay for your child to take his or her time when working
on these exercises.

■ Write a check mark (✓) above the picture that comes next in the
pattern.

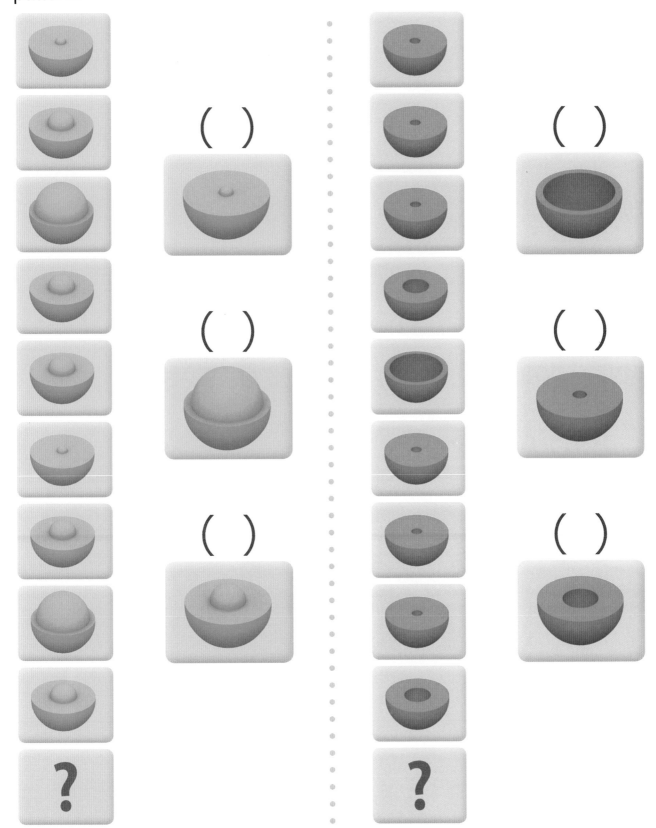

■ Write a check mark (✓) above the picture that comes next in the pattern.

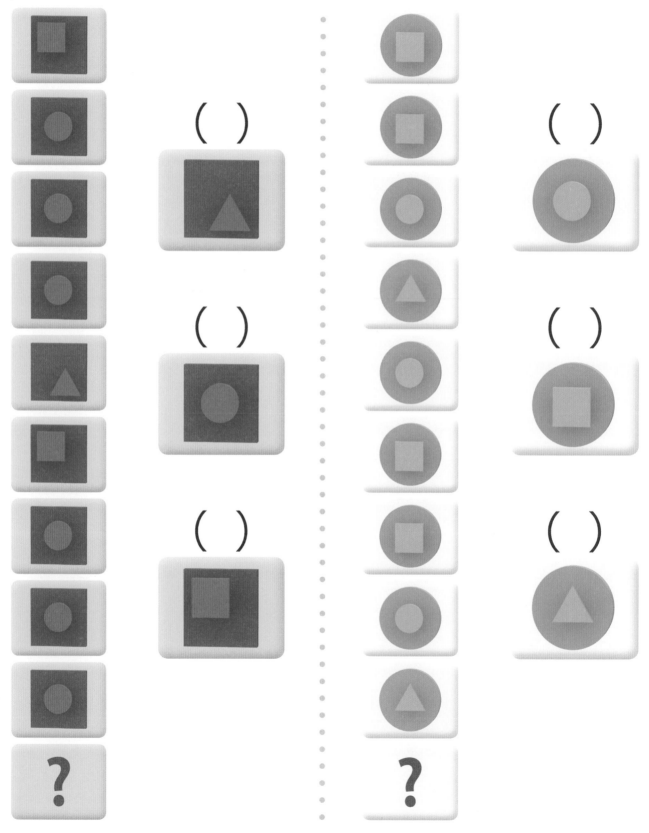

24

## Mazes
### Level One

Name

Date

**To parents**
Do the activities along with your child if he or she has difficulty. Make sure that your child draws only vertical and horizontal lines, not diagonal lines, to connect the pictures.

■ Draw a line from the arrow ( ➡ ) to the star ( ★ ), connecting only pansies ( ).

25

■ Draw a line from the arrow ( ➡ ) to the star ( ⭐ ), connecting only hamburgers ( 🍔 ).

## Mazes
### Level Two

Name

Date

**To parents**
If your child has difficulty, encourage him or her to identify the objects out loud as he or she finds the path through the maze.

■ Draw a line from the arrow ( ➡ ) to the star ( ★ ), connecting only boots ( 👢 ).

■ Draw a line from the arrow (➡) to the star (★), connecting only lions ( ).

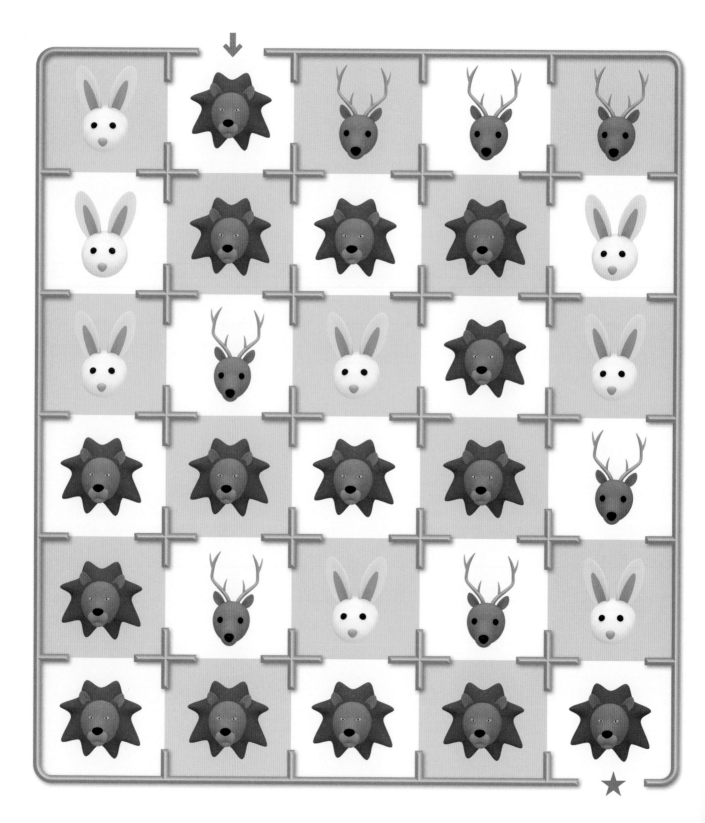

28

## Mazes
Level Three

Name

Date

**To parents**
If your child has difficulty, help him or her understand that the path through the maze now includes two kinds of pictures.

■ Draw a line from the arrow (➡) to the star (★), connecting only dandelions (🌼) and tulips (🌷).

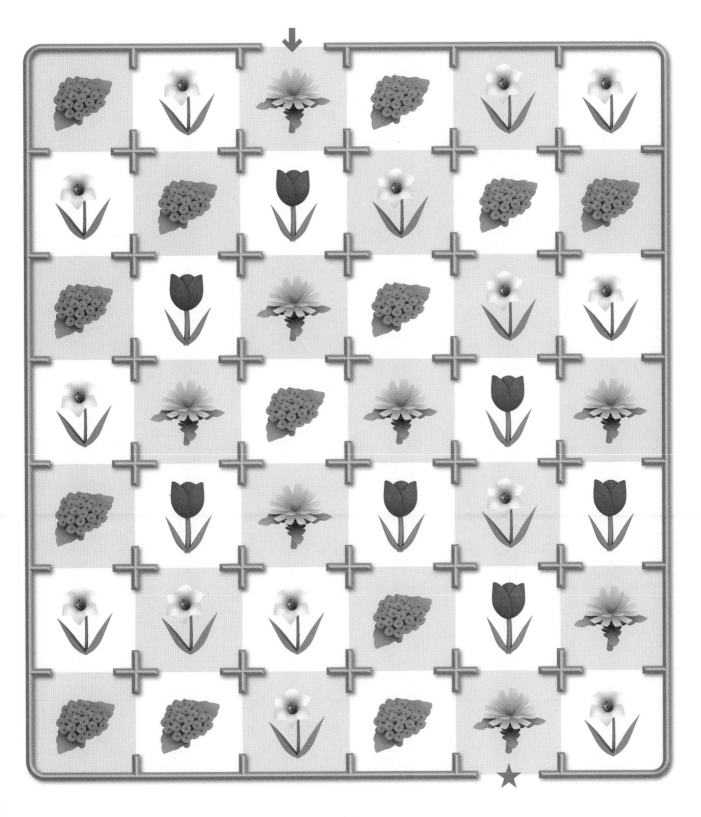

29

■ Draw a line from the arrow (➡) to the star (★), connecting only suns ( ☀ ) and moons ( 🌙 ).

## Mazes
### Level Four

Name

Date

**To parents**
Five kinds of pictures are now in the maze. Encourage your child to differentiate between the pictures.

■ Draw a line from the arrow (➡) to the star (★), connecting only balls ( ⚾ ) and bats ( 🏏 ).

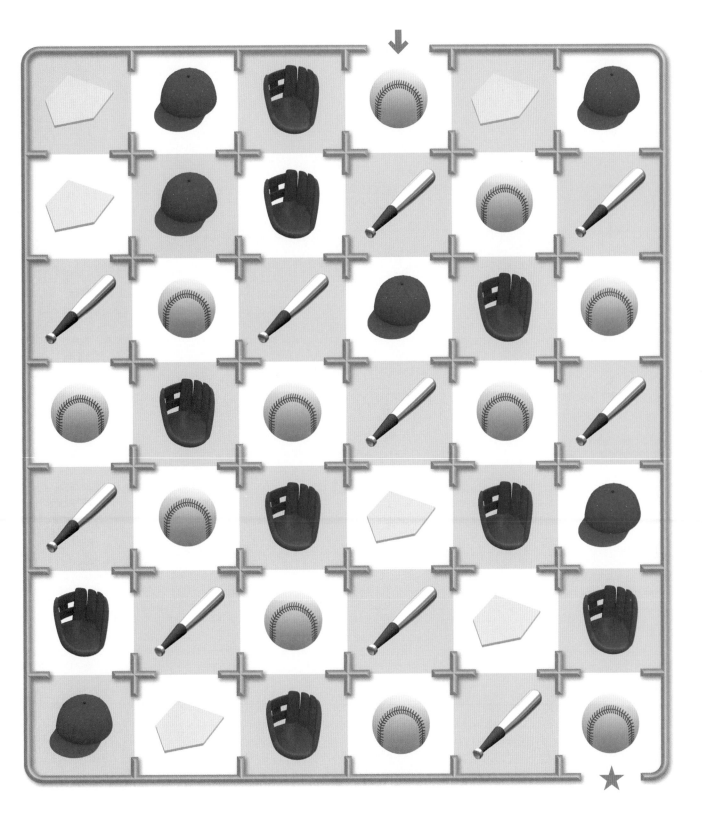

31

■ Draw a line from the arrow ( ➡ ) to the star ( ★ ), connecting only cows ( 🐄 ) and sheep ( 🐑 ).

## Mazes
### Level Five

Name

Date

**To parents**
If your child has difficulty, help him or her understand that the path through the maze now includes three kinds of pictures.

■ Draw a line from the arrow (➡) to the star (★), connecting only melons ( 🍈 ), grapes ( 🍇 ), and apples ( 🍎 ).

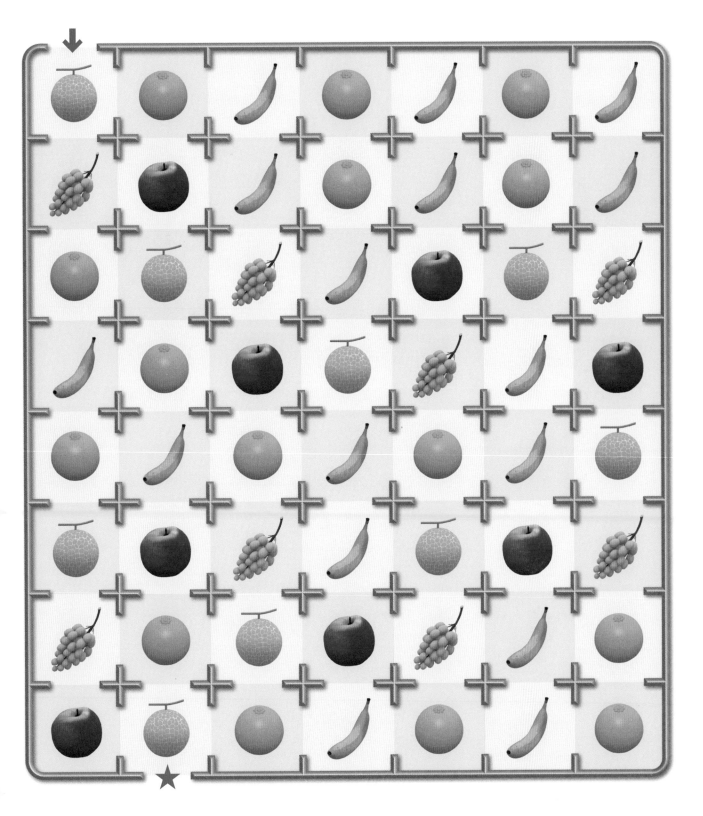

33

■ Draw a line from the arrow ( ➡ ) to the star ( ★ ), connecting only vests ( ), sweatshirts ( ), and T-shirts ( ).

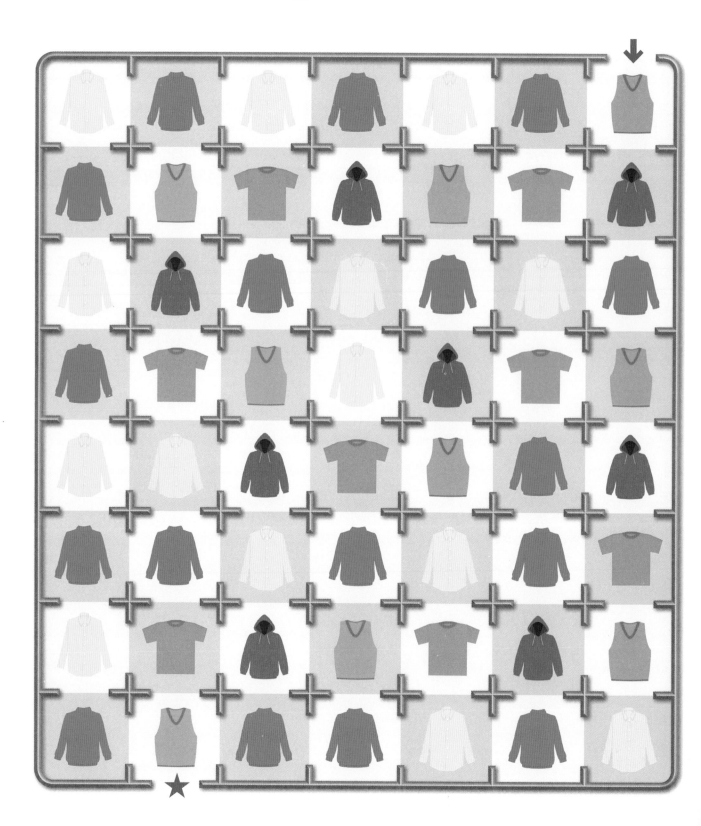

# Mazes
Level Six

Name

Date

**To parents**
Six kinds of pictures are now in the maze. Encourage your child to differentiate between the pictures.

■ Draw a line from the arrow ( → ) to the star ( ★ ), connecting only scissors ( ✂ ), highlighters ( ▮ ), and pencils ( ✏ ).

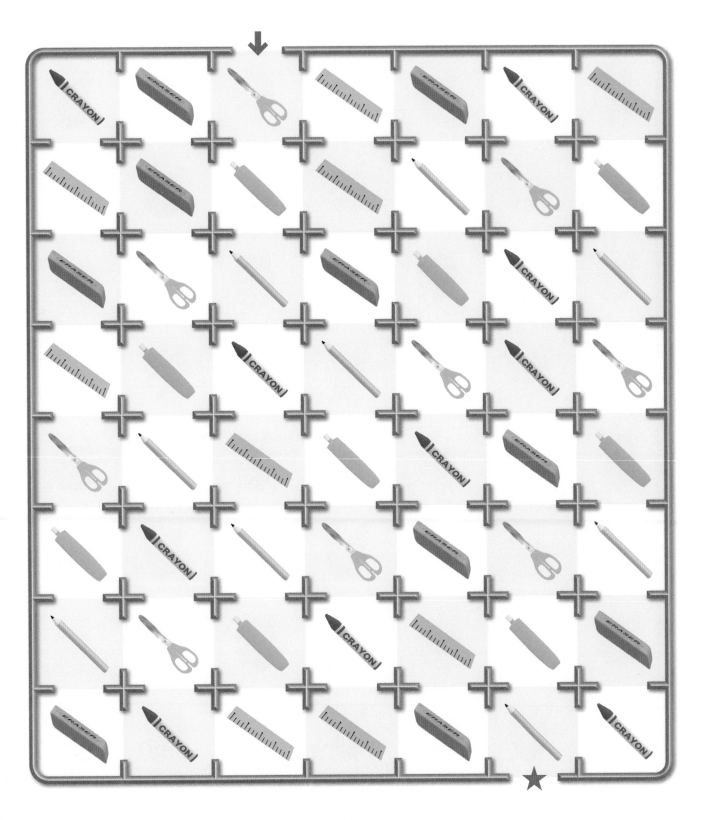

35

■ Draw a line from the arrow (➡) to the star (★), connecting only dogs ( 🐶 ), cats ( 🐱 ), and pigeons ( 🐦 ).

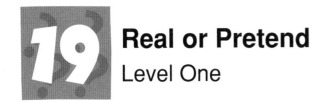

# Real or Pretend
Level One

■ Circle the three parts of the picture that are pretend.

■ Circle the three parts of the picture that are pretend.

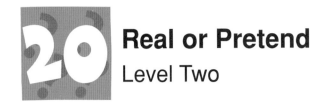

# Real or Pretend
Level Two

Name

Date

**To parents**
If your child has difficulty, ask him or her to describe the picture.

■ Circle the four parts of the picture that are pretend.

39

■ Circle the four parts of the picture that are pretend.

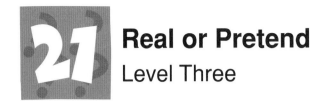

Name

Date

**To parents**
If your child has difficulty, ask him or her to find something in the picture that does not happen in real life.

■ Circle the five parts of the picture that are pretend.

■Circle the five parts of the picture that are pretend.

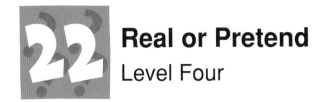

# 22 Real or Pretend
## Level Four

Name

Date

**To parents**
The number of pretend events has increased. Encourage your child to find all of them.

■ Circle the six parts of the picture that are pretend.

43

■ Circle the six parts of the picture that are pretend.

## Patterns with Rotating Blocks

One Quarter Turn

■ Write a check mark (✓) above the picture that comes next in the
pattern.

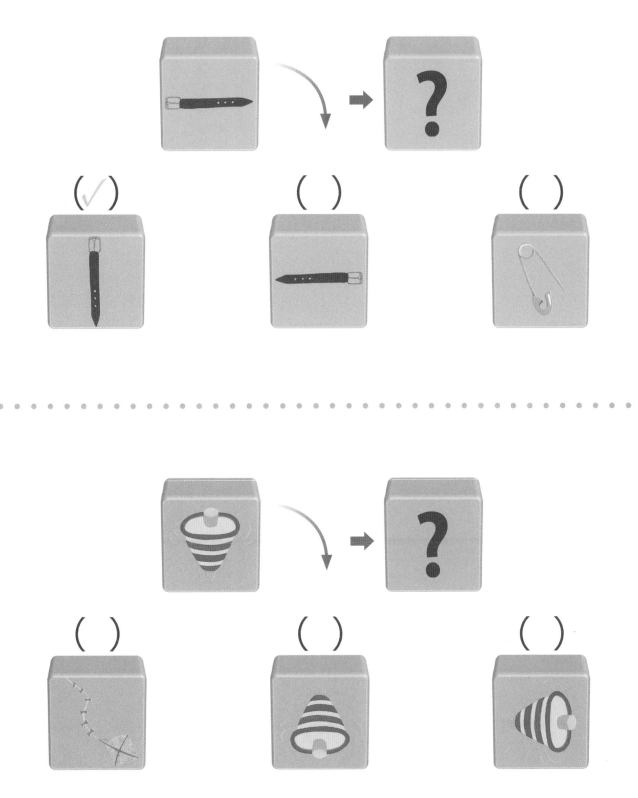

45

■ Write a check mark (✓) above the picture that comes next in the pattern.

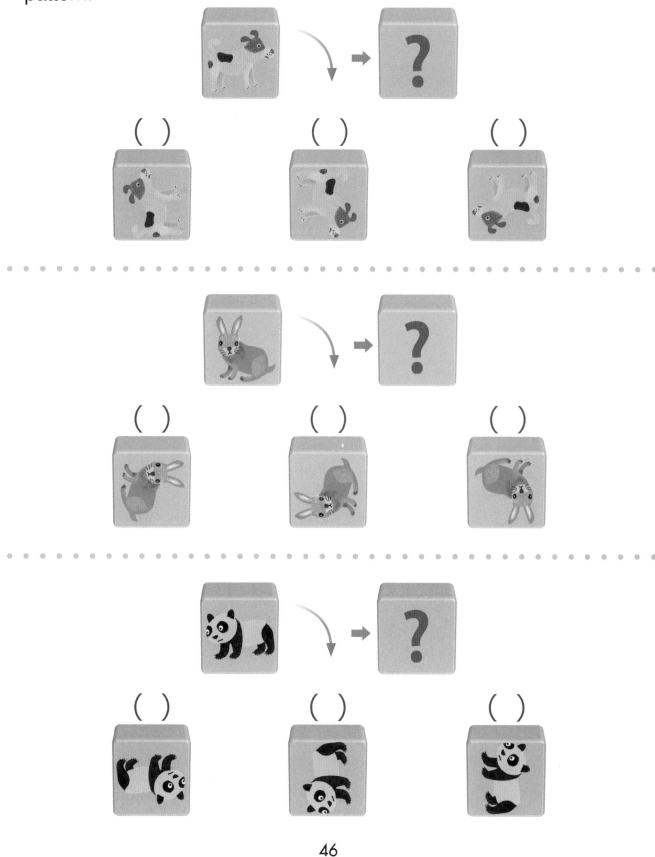

46

# Patterns with Rotating Blocks

## Two Quarter Turns

Name

Date

**To parents**
Help your child understand that the cube is upside down after
two quarter turns.

■ Write a check mark (✓) above the picture that comes next in the
pattern.

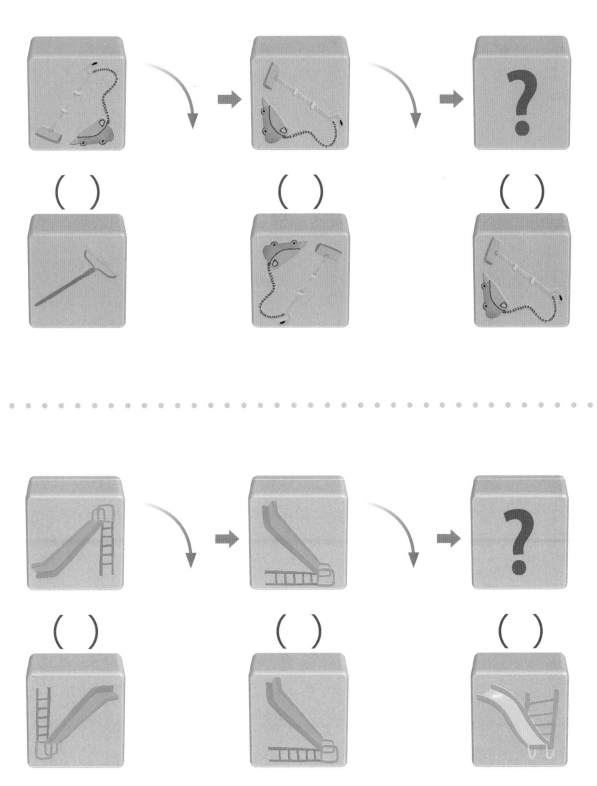

■ Write a check mark (✓) above the picture that comes next in the pattern.

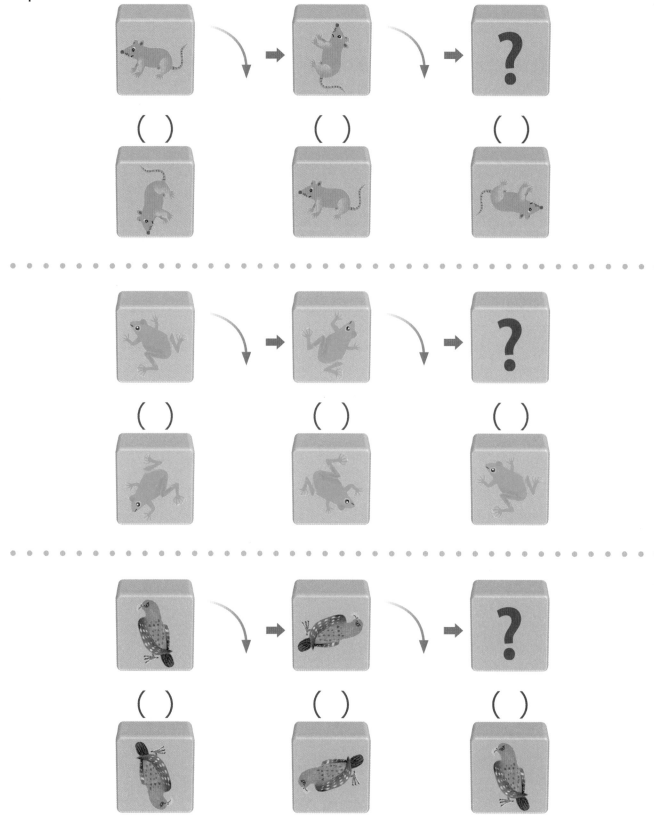

# Patterns with Rotating Blocks

## Three Quarter Turns

Name

Date

**To parents**
The cube has been rotated three quarter turns. If your child has difficulty, it may help to rotate this workbook three quarter turns.

■ Write a check mark (✓) above the picture that comes next in the pattern.

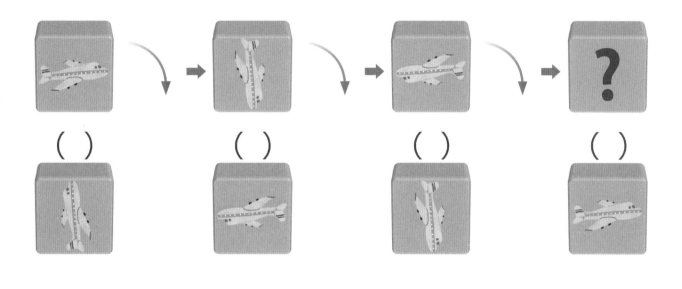

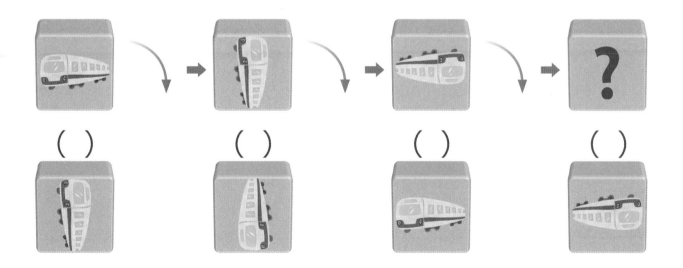

■ Write a check mark (✓) above the picture that comes next in the pattern.

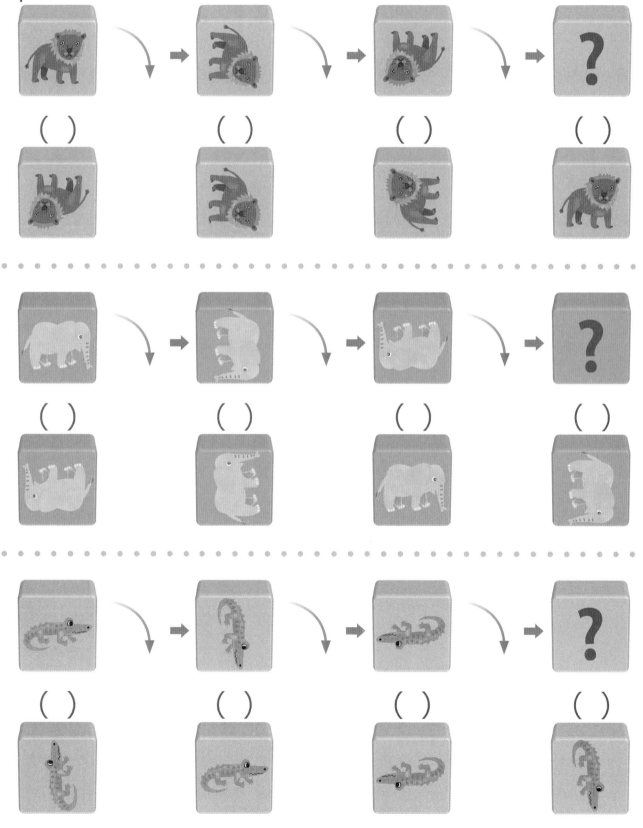

# Patterns with Rotating Blocks

## One to Three Quarter Turns

Name

Date

**To parents**
After this activity, you may wish to ask your child what the picture on a cube would look like after four quarter turns.

Write a check mark (✓) above the picture that comes next in the pattern.

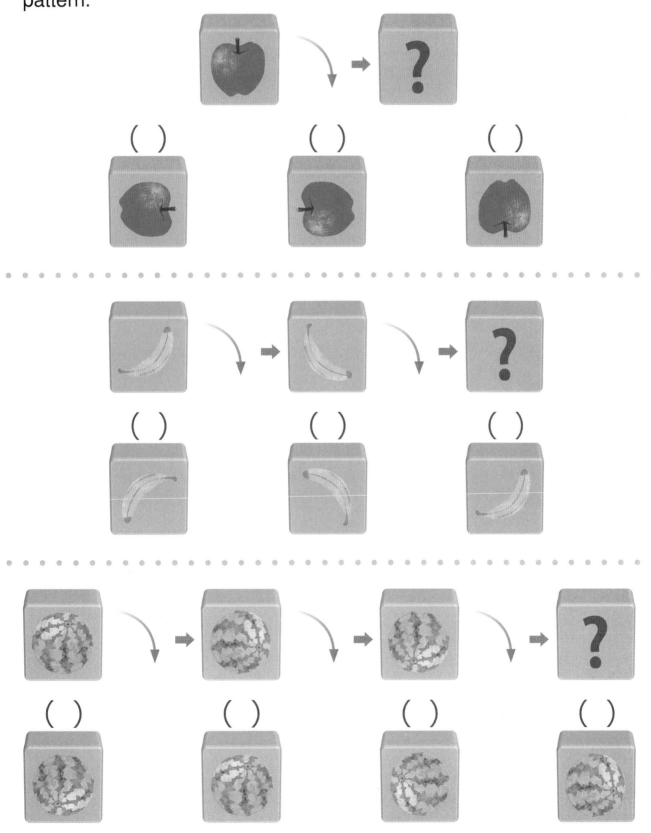

■ Write a check mark (✓) above the picture that comes next in the pattern.

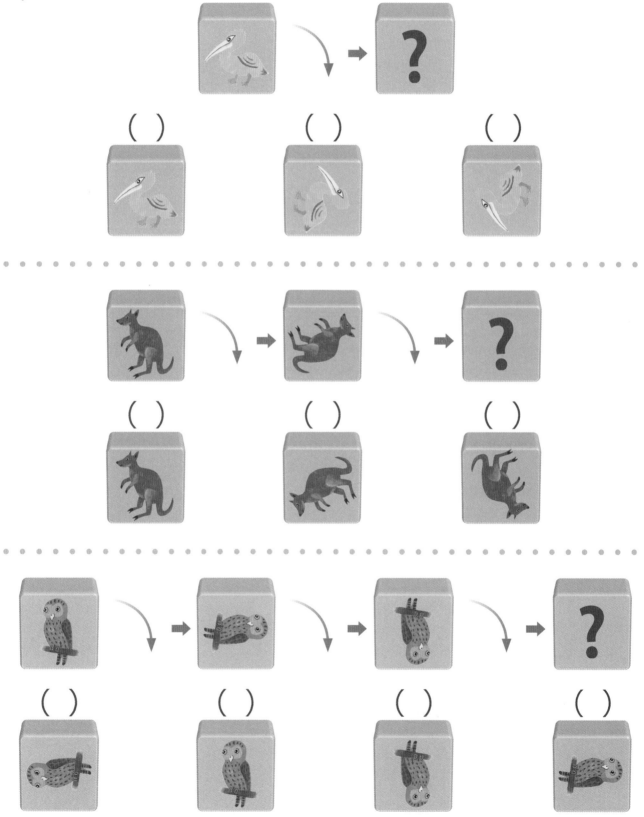

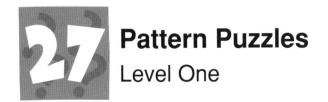

# Pattern Puzzles
## Level One

**To parents**
Guide your child to use the complete sequence shown in the top picture to choose the correct answer.

■ Write a check mark (✓) above the picture that shows the missing ball.

( ) ( ) ( ) ( ) ( )

■ Write a check mark (✓) above the picture that shows the missing animal.

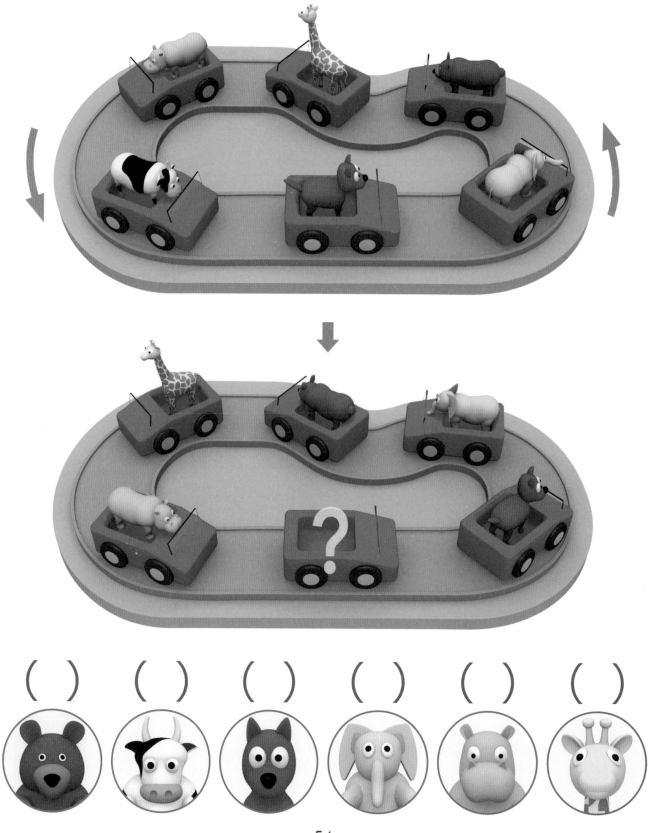

# Pattern Puzzles
## Level Two

Name

Date

**To parents**
If your child has difficulty, ask him or her how many positions an animal has moved.

■ Write a check mark (✓) above the picture that shows the missing animal.

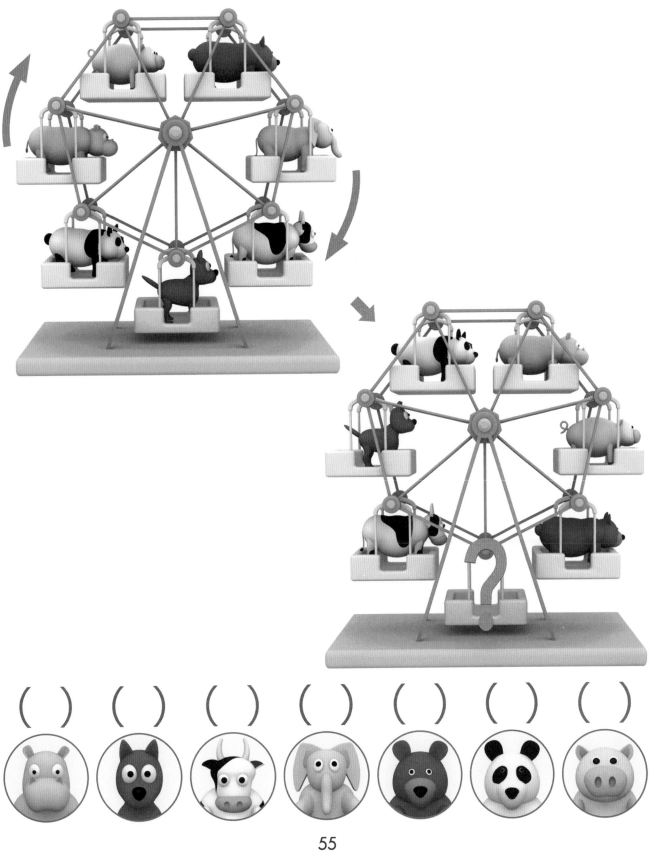

( )  ( )  ( )  ( )  ( )  ( )  ( )

■ Write a check mark (✓) above the picture that shows the missing animal.

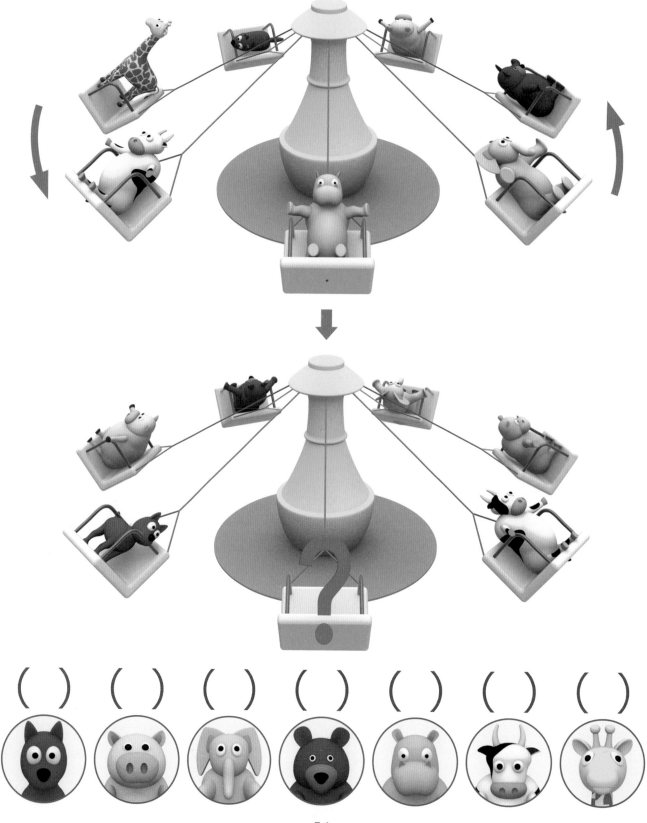

( )   ( )   ( )   ( )   ( )   ( )   ( )

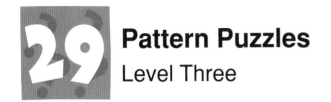
Name

Date

**To parents**
The activities are now more difficult because part of the sequence is hidden. Encourage your child to find a pattern.

■ Write a check mark (✓) above the picture that shows the missing ball.

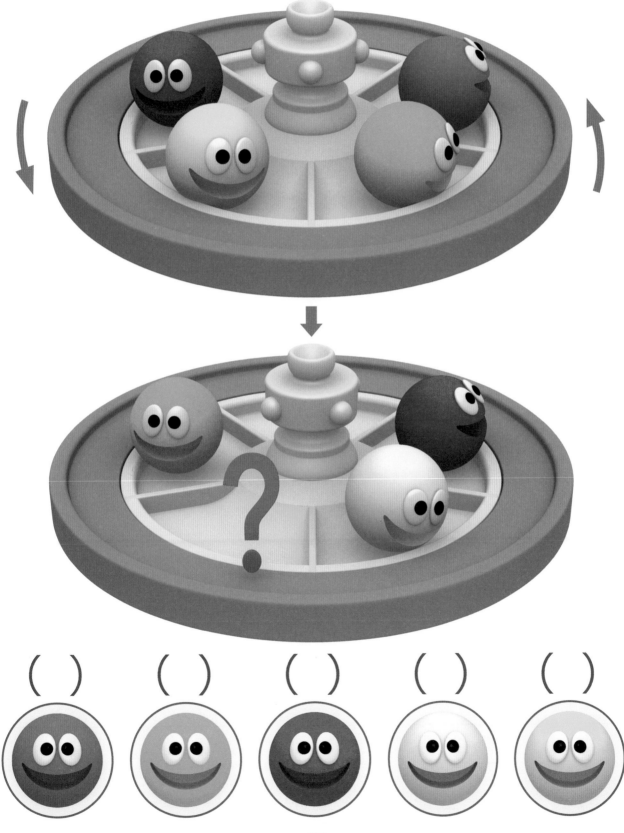

( )    ( )    ( )    ( )    ( )

57

■ Write a check mark (✓) above the picture that shows the missing animal.

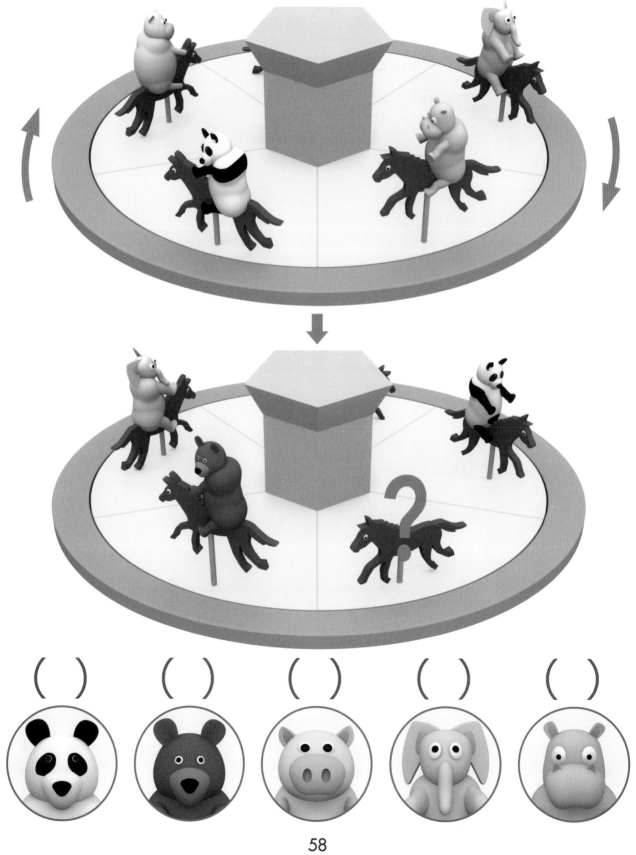

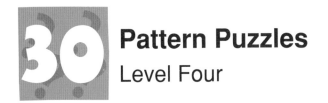

# Pattern Puzzles
## Level Four

Name

Date

**To parents**
To identify the missing animal, it may help to identify which animals are hidden.

■ Write a check mark (✓) above the picture that shows the missing animal.

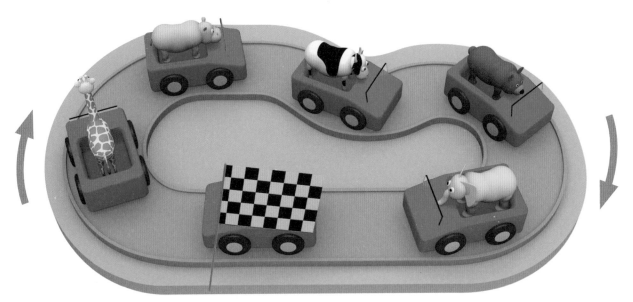

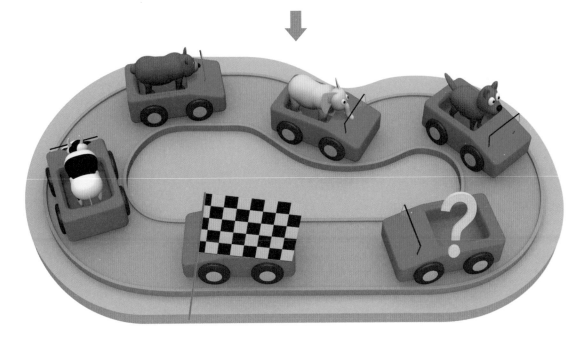

( )  ( )  ( )  ( )  ( )  ( )

■ Write a check mark (✓) above the picture that shows the missing animal.

# Pattern Puzzles
## Level Five

■ Write a check mark (✓) above the picture that shows the missing animal.

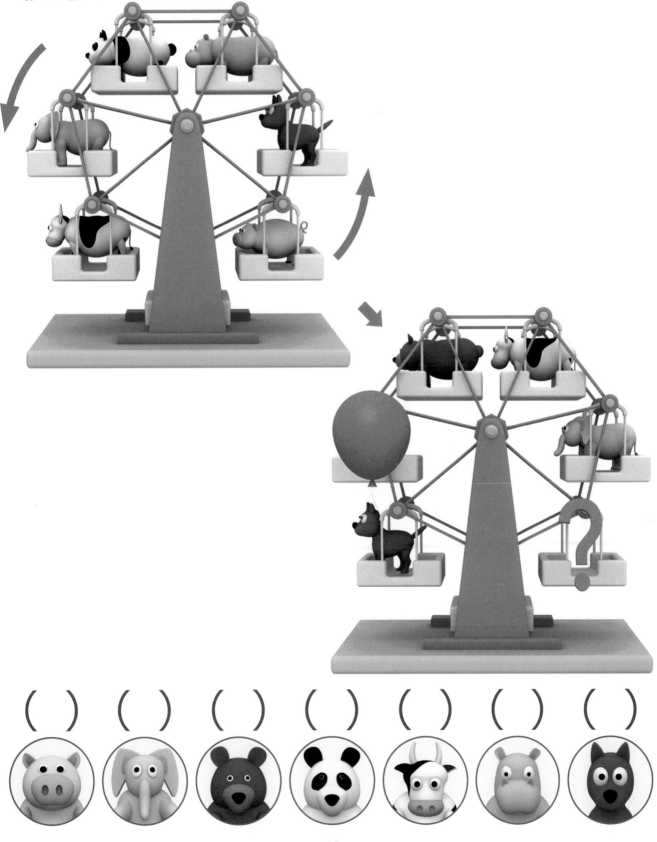

(  )   (  )   (  )   (  )   (  )   (  )   (  )

■ Write a check mark (✓) above the picture that shows the missing animal.

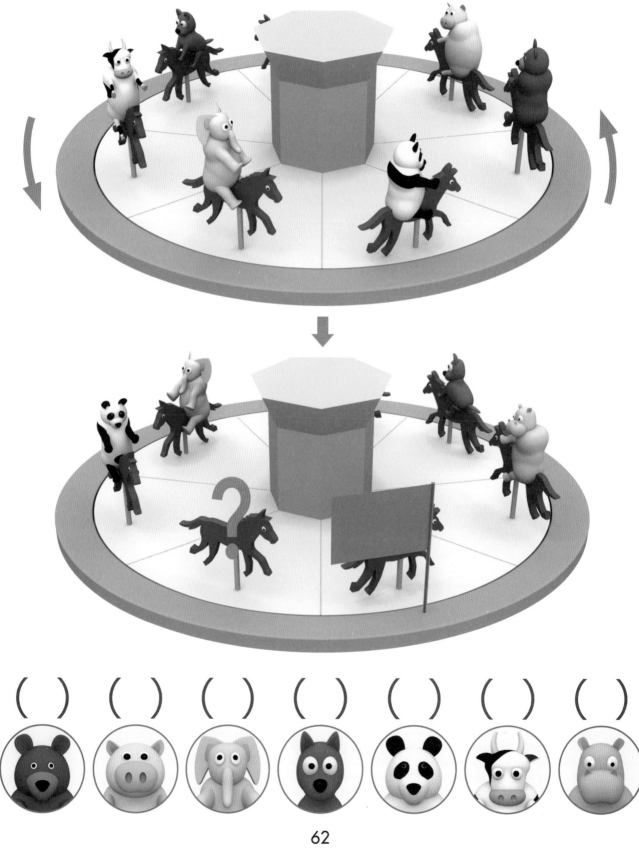

( )  ( )  ( )  ( )  ( )  ( )  ( )

# Pattern Puzzles
## Level Six

Name

Date

**To parents**
The number of animals has increased. If your child has difficulty, it may help for your child to count how many positions an animal has moved.

■ Write a check mark (✓) above the picture that shows the missing animal.

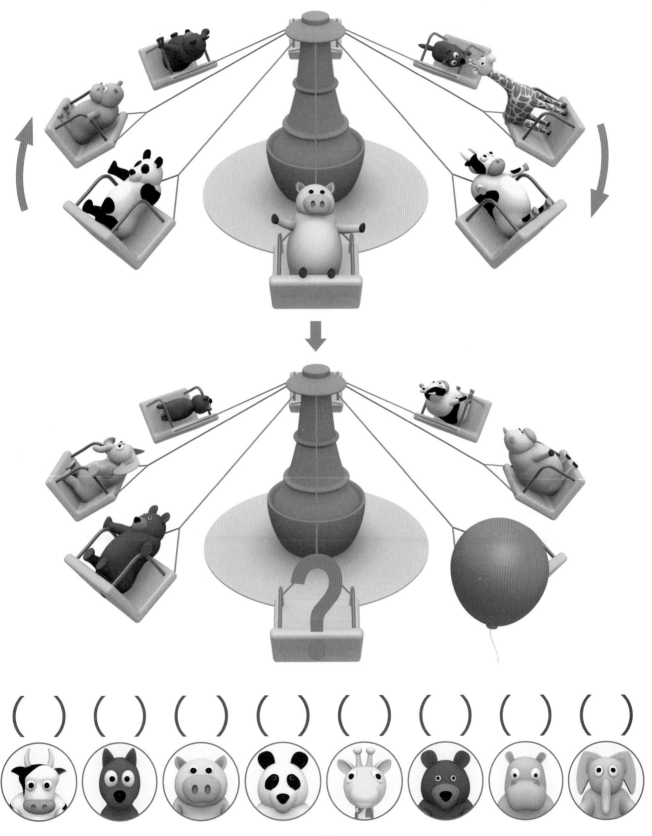

( ) ( ) ( ) ( ) ( ) ( ) ( ) ( )

■ Write a check mark (✓) above the picture that shows the missing animal.

( )　( )　( )　( )　( )　( )　( )　( )

# Color and Shape Patterns

## Level One

**To parents**
Colored pencils work best for these activities because the shape will remain visible after coloring.

■ Follow the pattern to color the picture in the margin.

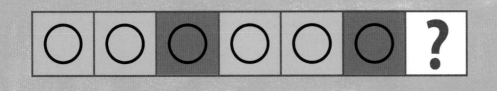

■ Follow the pattern to color the correct picture in the margin.

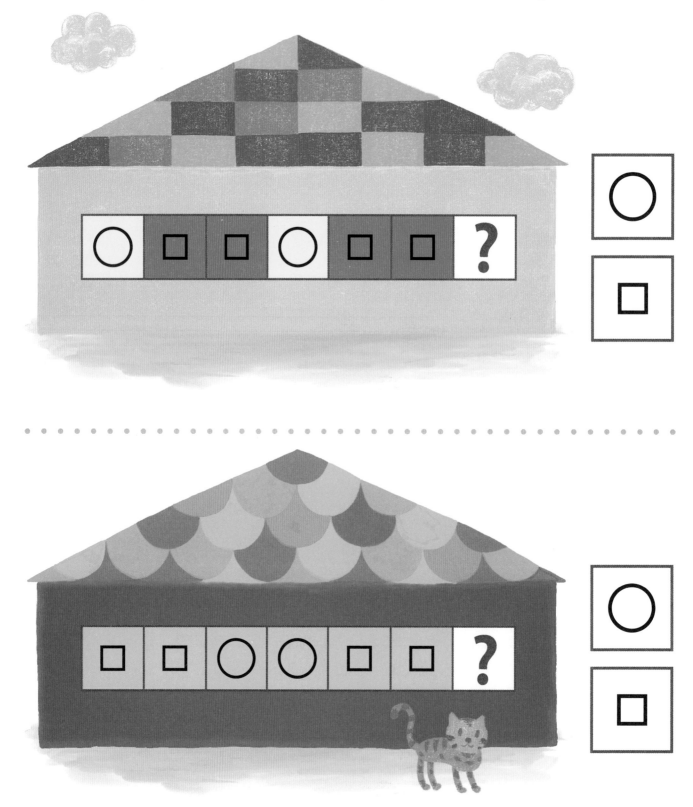

# Color and Shape Patterns
## Level Two

Name

Date

■ Follow the pattern to color the correct picture in the margin.

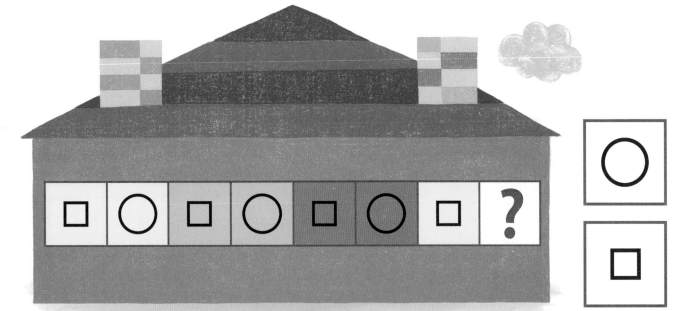

■ Follow the pattern to color the correct picture in the margin.

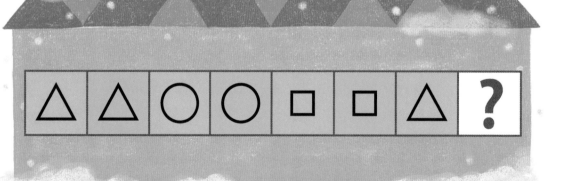

# Color and Shape Patterns

Level Three

Name

Date

**To parents**
The activities are now more difficult because part of the
sequence is hidden. Encourage your child to find a pattern.

■ Follow the pattern to color the picture in the margin.

■ Follow the pattern to color the correct picture in the margin.

# Color and Shape Patterns

## Level Four

**To parents**
For each pattern, the complete sequence is shown at least once.

■ Follow the pattern to color the correct picture in the margin.

**To parents**
This is the last exercise of this workbook. Please praise your
child for the effort it took to complete this workbook.

■ Follow the pattern to color the correct picture in the margin.

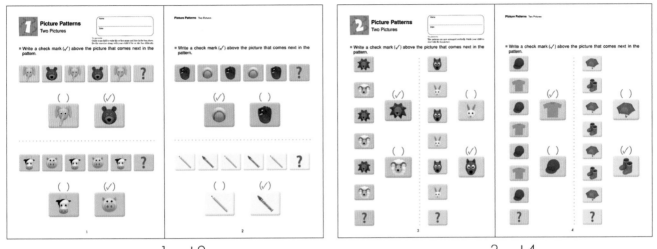

pages 1 and 2                    pages 3 and 4

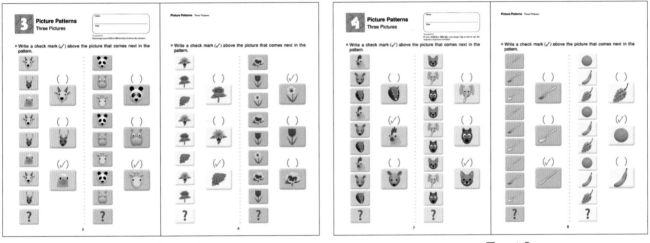

pages 5 and 6                    pages 7 and 8

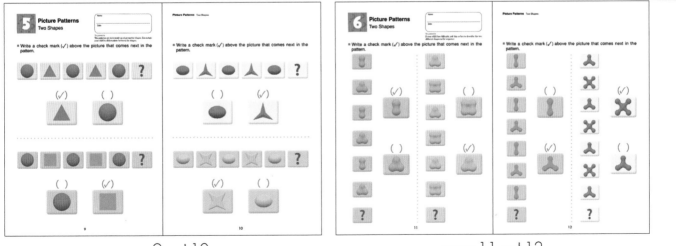

pages 9 and 10                   pages 11 and 12

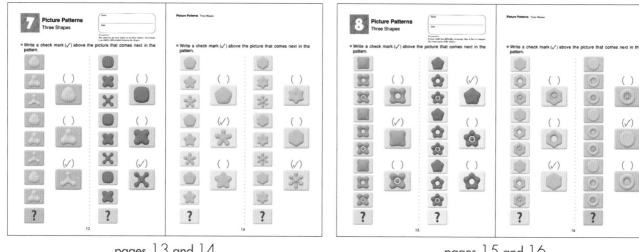

pages 13 and 14

pages 15 and 16

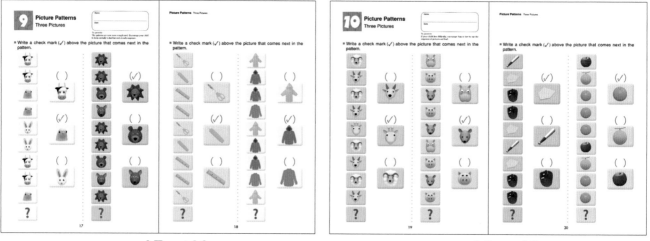

pages 17 and 18

pages 19 and 20

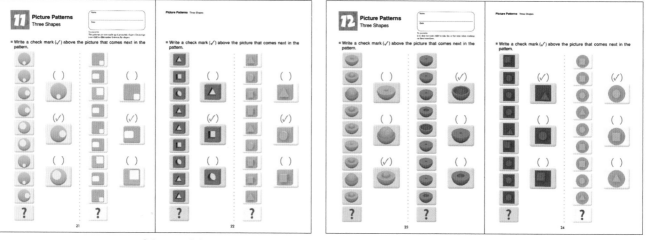

pages 21 and 22

pages 23 and 24

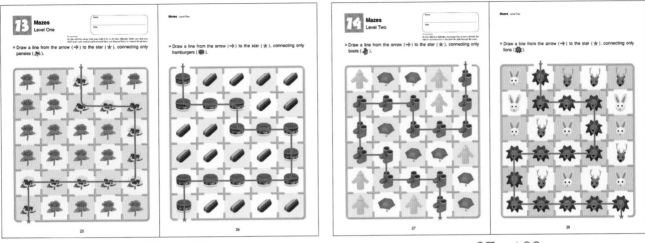

pages 25 and 26                    pages 27 and 28

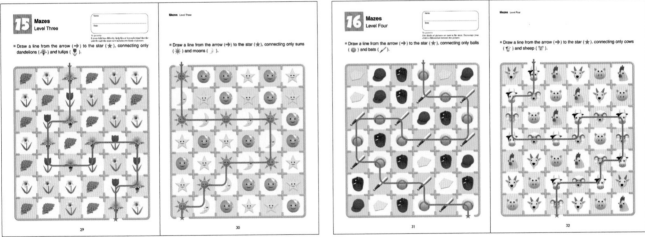

pages 29 and 30                    pages 31 and 32

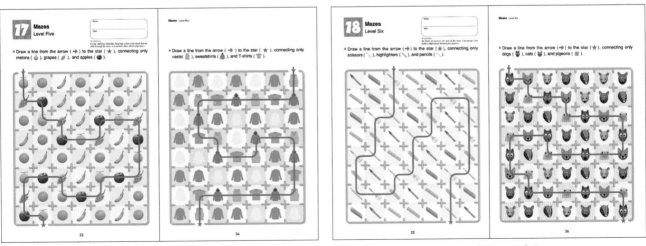

pages 33 and 34                    pages 35 and 36

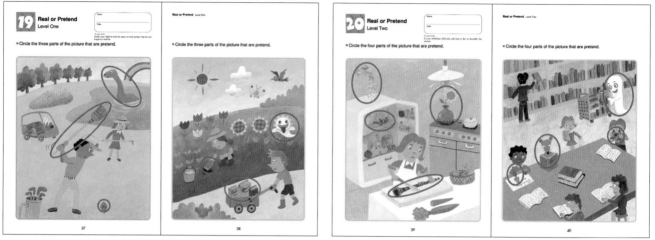

pages 37 and 38

pages 39 and 40

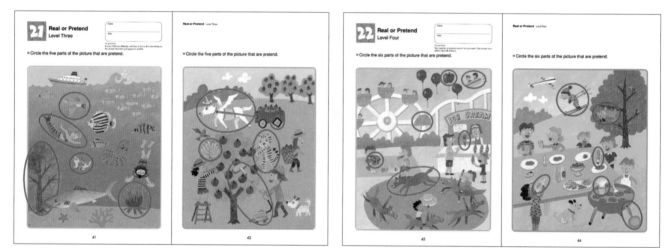

pages 41 and 42

pages 43 and 44

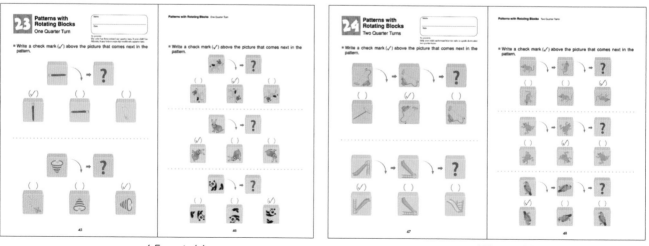

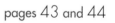

pages 45 and 46

pages 47 and 48

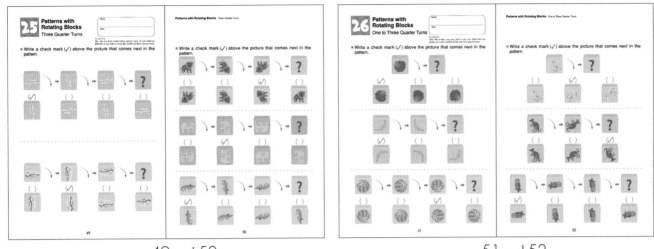

pages 49 and 50

pages 51 and 52

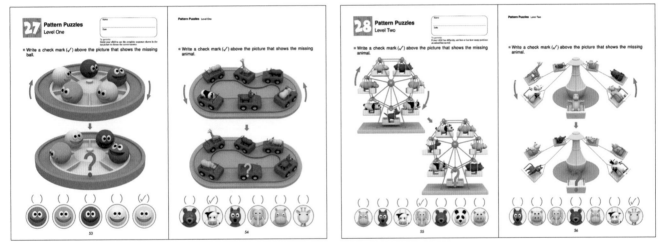

pages 53 and 54

pages 55 and 56

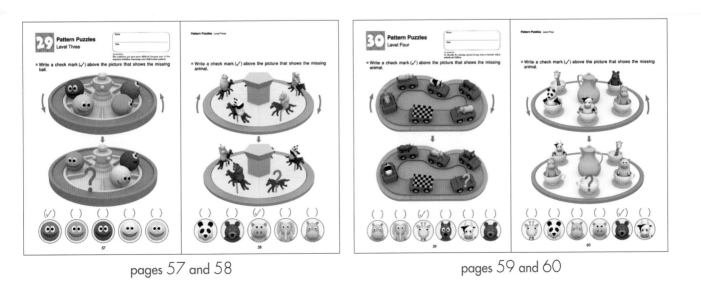

pages 57 and 58

pages 59 and 60

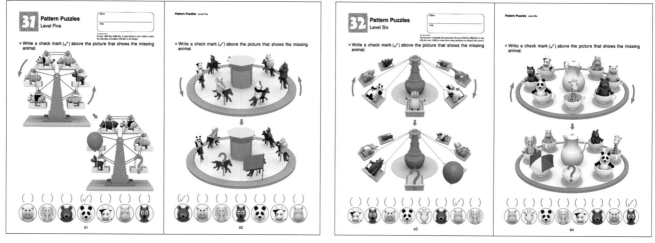

pages 61 and 62

pages 63 and 64

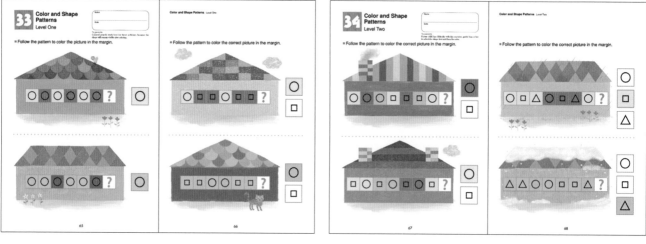

pages 65 and 66

pages 67 and 68

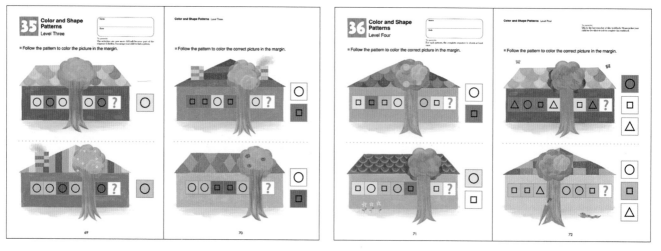

pages 69 and 70

pages 71 and 72

# Certificate of Achievement

KUM⊙N

is hereby congratulated on completing

## Thinking Skills Workbooks
## Kindergarten Logic

Presented on ............................. , 20 ..........

........................................

Parent or Guardian